Helping Children See Jesus

ISBN: 978-1-64104-037-2

GOD
His Son, His Book, His Home
New Testament Introductory Volume

Author: Ruth B. Greiner
Illustrator: Frances H. Hertzler
Computer Graphic Artist: Ed Olson
Typesetting and Layout: Morgan Melton, Patricia Pope

© 2018 Bible Visuals International
PO Box 153, Akron, PA 17501-0153
Phone: (717) 859-1131
www.biblevisuals.org

All rights reserved. No part of this publication may be reproduced, stored in a retrieval system or transmitted in any form by any means, electronic, mechanical, photocopy, recording or otherwise, without the prior permission of the publisher, except as provided by USA copyright law.

RELATED ITEMS

To access related items (such as activities, memory verse posters and translated texts) please visit our web store at www.biblevisuals.org and enter 1000 in the search box on the page.

FREE TEXT DOWNLOAD

To access a FREE printable copy of the teaching text (PDF format) in English or other available languages, enter S1000DL in the search box. Add the item to your cart, and use coupon code XTACSV17 at checkout. Once your order is processed you will receive an email with a link to the free download.

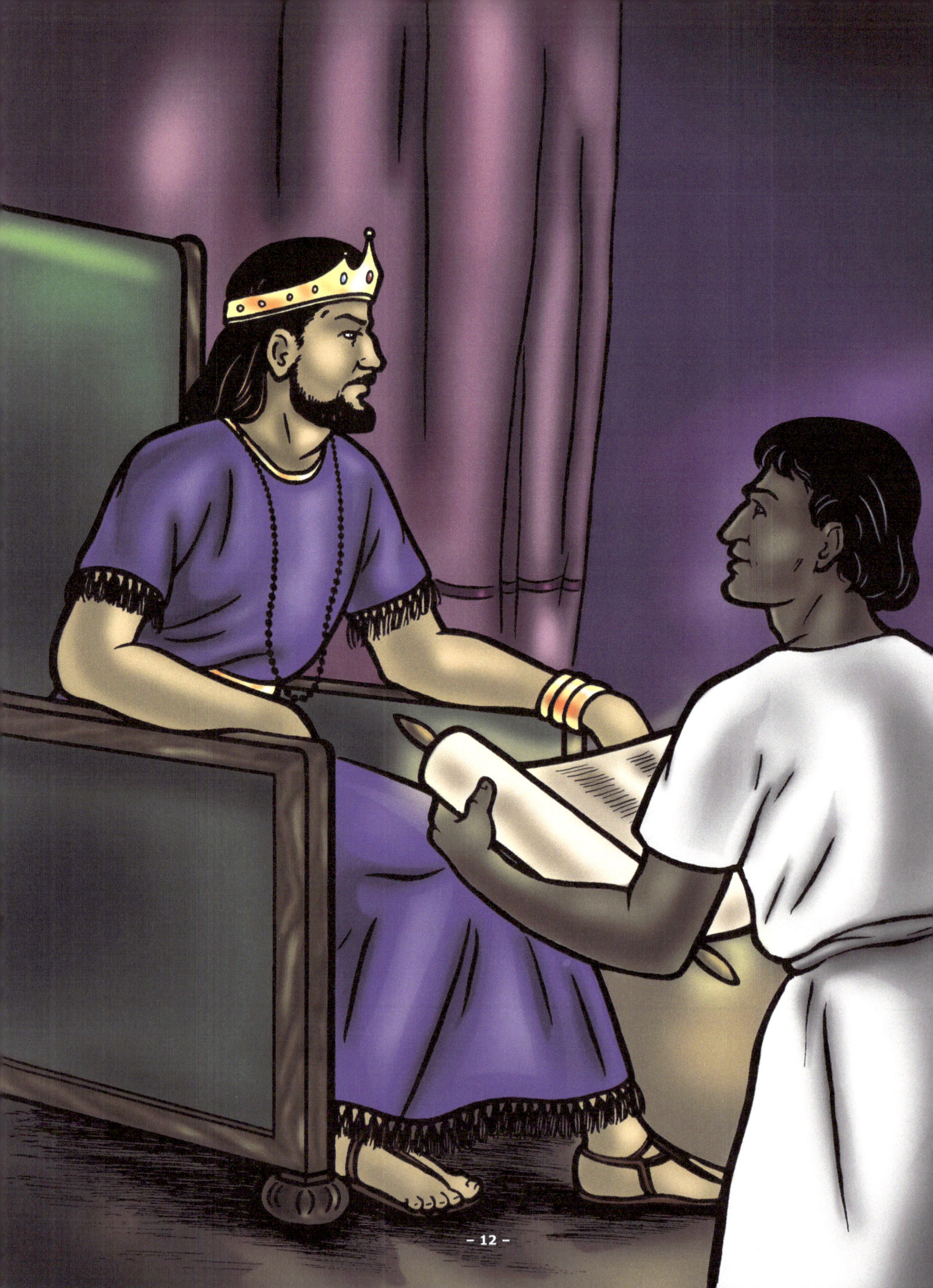

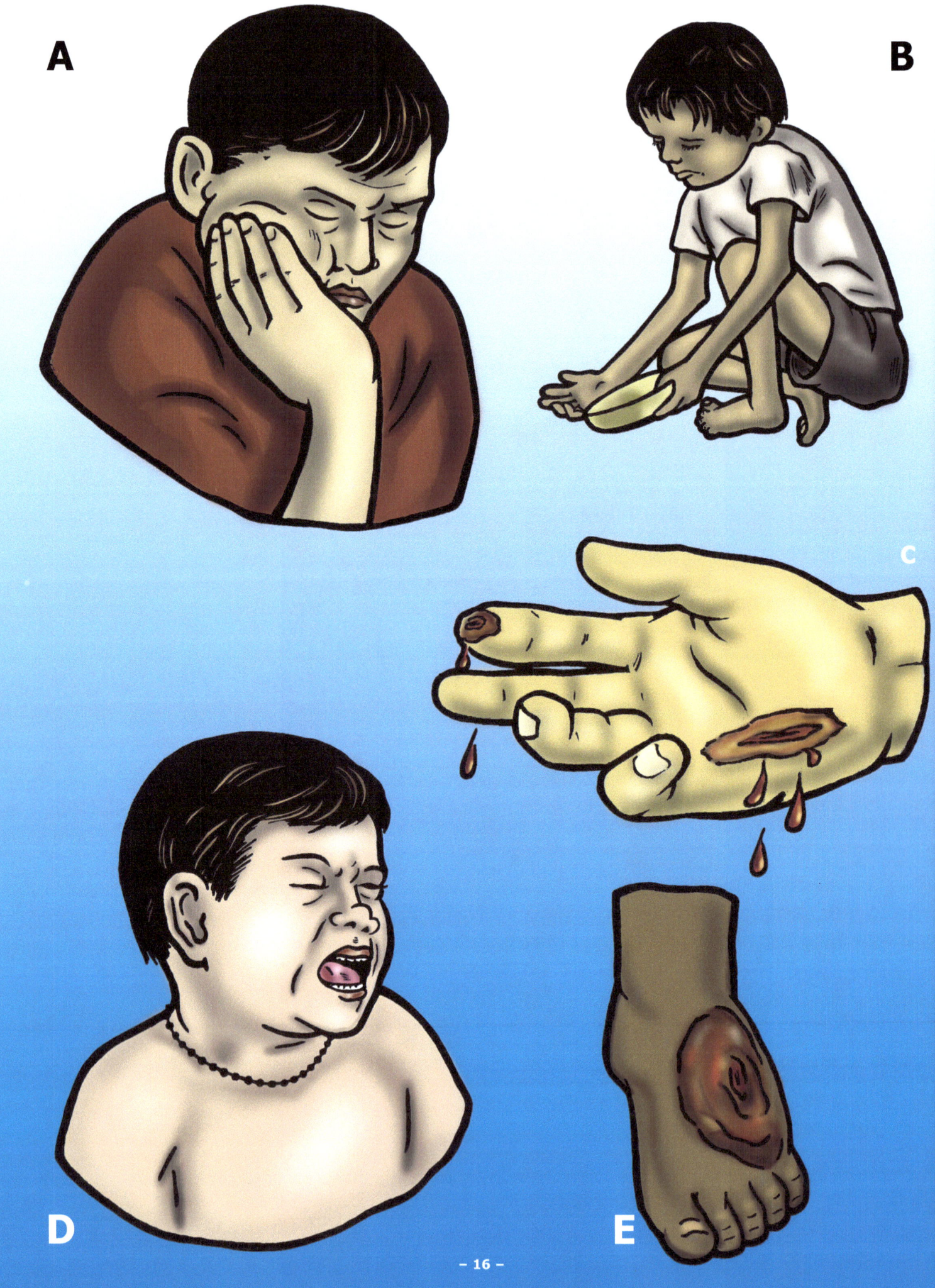

Ye turned to God from idols to serve the living and true God.
1 Thessalonians 1:9b

Lesson 1
GOD

Scripture to be studied: 1 Kings 18:17-39

The *aim* of the lesson: To help your students to know the only living and true God.

What your students should *know*: That God is the living and true God and He is personally interested in each individual.

What your students should *feel*: A desire to know more about God.

What your students should *do*: Think about God when they look at the trees and animals and people whom He created.

Lesson outline (for the teacher's and students' notebooks):

1. Idols cannot hear or answer prayer (1 Kings 18:17-35).
2. The living God hears prayer (1 Kings 18:36-37).
3. The living God answers prayer (1 Kings 18:38-39).
4. God the Creator is eternal, holy, and He is love (Genesis 1:1-31; Psalm 90:2; Leviticus 11:44; 1 John 4:8, 16).

NOTE TO THE TEACHER

You will enjoy teaching the four lessons in this volume, as well as all of the lessons in the volumes that follow.

Before reading the lesson as it is printed here, study 1 Kings 18:17-39 in your Bible. Once that event becomes alive to you, it will live to those whom you teach. Be sure to study carefully all of the Bible verses mentioned in all of the lesson material.

Throughout all four of the lessons in this series, teach this verse:

Ye turned to God from idols to serve the living and true God. (1 Thessalonians 1:9b)

THE LESSON

Have you ever looked at things around you and asked, "Where did they come from? How did the trees, the sky, the water, animals, and people come into being?"

The answer is simply this: All things were made by Him who has all power. His name is *God*.

When we look at a house, we know that someone planned it and built it. Could a house appear out of a heap of things thrown together on a pile? Certainly not! Nor could this world simply happen. God planned every bit of it and, in the beginning, it was perfect. God made it all–and He made it out of nothing! God made *you*–He made all people everywhere. He is the One who put life into you.

Maybe you are wondering, *But who made God? When did God come into being?*

The answer is: God always was. And God always will be. (See Psalm 90:2.) Even if you do not understand this, it is true. By the time you are finished studying these lessons, you will know more about the living and true God. You will learn about His Son, His Book, and His home where He wants you to live with Him. Though we may not *understand* these things, we can *believe* them. And if we believe them, God will help us to know more about Him.

1. IDOLS CANNOT HEAR OR ANSWER PRAYER
1 Kings 18:17-35

There are some people who believe that the sun in the sky is a god. Others believe the moon and the stars are gods. (See 2 Kings 23:5.) Still others believe a god can be made of wood or stone, silver or gold. (See Psalm 115:4-8.)

Can these things be the living and true God? Can the sun hear your prayers? Can the moon or stars see you and help you? No!

Idols carved from wood or stone may have eyes. But they cannot see you. Gods made of gold and silver may have ears. But they cannot hear you. The hands of those idols cannot move to help you. For such gods are made by man.

Do you know the only God who *can* see you, the One who *can* hear you, the One who *can* help you, the only God who made you? Our lesson will tell us about Him.

There was in the long, long ago, a man named Elijah. He lived among people who worshiped a god of their own. They named their god *Baal*. They believed Baal could help them. But Elijah did not believe in Baal. He believed in the living and true God.

One day Elijah called together 450 of the followers (prophets) of Baal. "Let us build an altar and offer a sacrifice," Elijah said. (An altar was often made of stones piled upon each other, with wood on top. It has always been the plan of God that a person who sins [does wrong things] must be punished. The punishment is death. At the time of Elijah, God would accept an animal substitute. The animal substitute was known as a *sacrifice*. Its life was given in place of the life of the sinner.)

After telling the followers of Baal to build an altar and offer a sacrifice, Elijah continued, "We will not put any fire under the sacrifice. Then you call to Baal and ask him to send fire to burn up the sacrifice. After that, I will call on my God to send fire. The One who sends the fire is the living and true God."

Show Illustration #1

The people agreed to the test. They placed the animal (bullock) on their altar. Then they prayed to their god to send fire and burn up the sacrifice. "Oh, Baal, hear us!" they cried. They jumped upon the altar, crying loudly for Baal to hear them. They cut themselves with knives, hoping that their god would then listen to them. Hour after hour they cried. All day they shouted. By evening their voices were too tired to cry out anymore. But nothing had happened. The god they had made (Baal) had not heard them.

Then it was Elijah's turn. He used 12 stones and built an altar in the name of God. He made a trench about the altar. He put the wood in order, cut the animal in pieces, and laid it on the wood. Then, strangely, he commanded: "Fill four barrels [large, earthen pots] with water and pour it on the sacrifice and on the wood." His command was obeyed.

"Do it again," he ordered. They did it again. "Now do it again!" Altogether twelve barrels of water were poured onto the altar. Surely no ordinary fire could burn up that wet sacrifice!

– 18 –

2. THE LIVING GOD HEARS PRAYER
1 Kings 18:36-37

Show Illustration #2

Then Elijah walked close to the altar. He prayed, "Lord God . . . let it be known this day that You are God . . . Hear me, O Lord, hear me, that this people may know that You are the Lord God."

3. THE LIVING GOD ANSWERS PRAYER
1 Kings 18:38-39

Show Illustration #3

Immediately fire fell from Heaven. It burned the sacrifice and the wood and the stones and the dust, and it licked up the water all around the altar! The living and true God had answered prayer.

When the followers of Baal saw what had happened, they fell down on their faces and cried, "The Lord, He is the God; the Lord, He is the God."

He is indeed the living and true God, the One who can hear when you talk to Him (pray), the One who sees everything you do. He is the One who made you. And He loves you!

4. GOD THE CREATOR IS ETERNAL, HOLY, AND HE IS LOVE
Genesis 1:1-31; Psalm 90:2; Leviticus 11:44; 1 John 4:8, 16

Because He loves you, you are going to want to know all that you can about Him. From our lesson today, there are four things that you should remember. (There is much, much more to know. And, if you attend class without fail, you will learn a great deal about God–and about many other things.) So that you will not forget these truths, why not write them in a notebook? Then you can read them every day. Soon you will find that you have remembered them. Then, when you want to tell others about the living and true God, you will be able to say:

Show Illustration #4a

1. God is *Creator*. (See Genesis 1.)

The living and true God is the One who made this world, the trees, the sky, the water, and animals. He made the sun and moon and stars. He is the One who made all people everywhere. God made it all and made it out of nothing. He spoke and it was so. He, *the maker of all things*, is known as the *Creator*.

Show Illustration #4b

2. God is *Eternal*. (See Psalm 90:2.)

"Eternal" means *without beginning or ending*. (The circle in the drawing has no beginning or ending. Trace it with your finger as you speak, teacher.) The living and true God has always been. He always will be. Before the worlds were, God was. Forever and forever and forever, God will be. *God, the Creator, is the Eternal One.*

Show Illustration #4c

3. God is *Holy*. (See Leviticus 11:44; Isaiah 6:3; Isaiah 57:15; 1 Peter 1:16.)

When we speak of God as being *holy*, we mean that He is perfect. (The white circle against the dark background helps us to remember that God is holy, pure, perfect.) Because God is perfect, He is without sin. He has never done one wrong thing. God hates sin. Yet all people everywhere continually do wrong things. It is God's plan that if sinning people are to be forgiven, a sacrifice must be made. Something–or Someone–will have to suffer the punishment for our sin. That punishment is death.

Show Illustration #4d

4. God is *Love*. (See 1 John 4:8, 16.)

The living and true God who made you, the One who always was and who always will be, the perfect, holy One, loves you! He loves you with all His heart. Because He knew that you would sin, He planned a way (long, long before you were ever born) for you to have your sin forgiven. He caused One, His only Son, to take your death penalty.

When Elijah lived, God accepted an animal sacrifice. Uncounted thousands of animals died, each taking the place of a sinful person. No longer are animal sacrifices needed. Nor will God accept animal sacrifices today. His only Son, about whom we will learn in our next lesson, died on a cross once for all people everywhere. Only if we believe in the living and true God, only if we believe that His Son took the punishment for our sins, can we be forgiven of our sin. Why did the eternal, holy God cause His Son to die? Because He loves *you*. *God is Love!*

There is much, much more to know about the living and true God. But between now and our next class, do this: Each time you look at a flower or a tree, the sun, the moon and stars, say to yourself, "God made that. Before there was ever a lake or a man, God was. God always will be. God is perfect. I have done wrong things. That means I am a sinner. And God hates sin. But God is love. God loves me. He caused His Son to die in my place."

Say those things again and again. Then, in our next lesson, we will learn about the Son of God–the One who took the punishment of death in our place.

NOTE TO THE TEACHER

If you feel that there is more in this lesson than your pupils can understand, divide it and make two lessons.

If you teach with conviction, your students will know that you yourself believe that the One of whom you speak is indeed the living and true God.

It is suggested that in their notebooks (which all members of your class should have) they should write the four main points of the lesson. Or, if they prefer, have them make four simple drawings like those on illustration #4. This will help them to remember the lesson.

Lesson 2
THE SON OF GOD

Scripture to be studied: All verses mentioned in the text.

The *aim* of the lesson: To show that Jesus Christ is the Son of God, who, because of His great love, took the punishment for our sins.

What your students should *know*: Jesus Christ loves them and died for their sins.

What your students should *feel*: Grateful for His love.

What your students should *do*: Throughout the week, repeat to themselves: "The Lord Jesus, the Son of God, loves me. He died for me. He wants me to believe in Him and receive Him."

Lesson outline (for the teacher's and students' notebooks):

1. The Son of God came to earth as a baby (Luke 2:1-12).
2. The Son of God died, taking all our sins on Himself (1 Peter 2:24).
3. Christ proved He is the Son of God by rising from the dead (1 Corinthians 15:3-4).
4. Christ went up in the clouds to be with God the Father (Acts 1:9-11).

NOTE TO THE TEACHER

One of the most important laws of teaching is:

Review, review, review.

This is especially necessary when teaching the truths of the Word of God. Much–perhaps all–that is in these lessons is new to your pupils. It is not enough simply to *tell* the lessons. The learners must understand what you are teaching. Remember that you are not teaching *lessons*; you are teaching *people*. Give them opportunities to ask questions. If there is more here than can be understood in one lesson, divide it into two lessons. May the Book and its glorious message live to you, dear teacher! Then it will live to your pupils.

Keep this verse before your class:

Ye turned to God from idols to serve the living and true God. **(1 Thessalonians 1:9b)**

THE LESSON

Since our last lesson, you have been thinking about God. You have thought of Him when you looked at the trees and animals and people. You have thought:

God made all of these things. *He is the Creator.*
God is eternal. He always was. He always will be.
God is holy. He has no sin. He hates sin (the wrong things people do).
God is love. God loves me!

As you have thought about these things, you may have wondered, What is God like? Where is God? How can I know more about Him? Our lesson today will help you to know the answers to these questions.

1. THE SON OF GOD CAME TO EARTH AS A BABY
Luke 2:1-12

Show Illustration #5

God knew that you would wonder about Him. He knew that you might find it hard to believe in One who has never been seen. (See John 1:18.) One day (over 2,000 years ago) God sent His Son to this world. His Son is named the Lord Jesus Christ. While He was here on earth, the Lord Jesus said, "He that hath seen Me, hath seen the Father [God]" (John 14:9). Because the Son of God lived here for many years (33), He was seen by uncounted numbers of people. God caused a record to be kept in a Book (the Bible)–a record which tells us about Him and His Son, the Lord Jesus Christ. (We will learn about that Book in our next lesson.)

Since the Son of God is like God the Father, you already know four things about the Son of God. What are they?

Like God the Father, *the Son of God is the Creator of all things*. We are told: "All things were made by Him [the Son of God]; and without Him was not any thing made that was made" (John 1:3).

God the Father said of His Son, "Thou, Lord, in the beginning hast laid the foundation of the earth; and the heavens are the works of Thine hands" (Hebrews 1:10).

We are told that the Son of God "is the image of the invisible God . . . For by Him [the Son of God] were all things created, that are in Heaven, and that are in earth . . . all things were created by Him . . . He is before all things" (Colossians 1:15-17).

This helps us to know that, like God the Father, *the Son of God is eternal.* He always was; He always will be. God and His Son, the Lord Jesus Christ, were together before the worlds were ever made.

Not only is the Lord Jesus the *Creator*, not only is He eternal, but He is like God in another way: He is *holy*. (See Luke 1:35; Romans 1:4.) Never, never did the Lord Jesus do or say or think one wrong thing. (See 2 Corinthians 5:21; 1 Peter 2:22.) He is perfect. So, like His Father, He hates the wrong things (sins) which people do.

By now you have remembered the fourth way in which the Lord Jesus and God are alike. *The Lord Jesus loves you.* (See 2 Corinthians 5:14; 1 John 4:19; Revelation 1:5.) He proved His love in a most unusual way. When you learn what He did, you should love Him with all your heart.

When the Lord Jesus Christ left His home with God the Father, He came to earth as a baby. *How* He came was a miracle. (We will learn more about that in the next series.) So that men would not think that an ordinary baby had been born, God caused the skies to open, and angels (who are the servants of God in the heavens) announced that the Son of God was born.

When the Lord Jesus was a man, God again opened the heavens. And God Himself said of His Son, "This is My beloved Son, in Whom I am well pleased" (Matthew 3:17). Another time God spoke from a cloud, saying, "This is My beloved Son, in Whom I am well pleased; hear ye Him" (Matthew 17:5).

The Lord Jesus said, "I and My Father are one" (John 10:30). That He and God are one was proved by the amazing things He said and the miracles that He did. He did so many things that, if they should be written every one, even the world itself is probably not big enough to contain all the books that could be written! (See John 21:25.) We are going to learn about some of the things the Lord Jesus did in the lessons which follow. We will learn how He, the Son of God on earth, caused a storm to stop by speaking to the wind. He healed the blind simply by speaking a word. He made sick people well. More than once He raised dead people and brought them back to life. How did He do it? He simply spoke, and it was so.

Why did the Lord Jesus leave His home with God the Father? Because God wanted us to know what He Himself is like.

2. THE SON OF GOD DIED, TAKING ALL OUR SINS ON HIMSELF
1 Peter 2:24

But there is another reason for the coming of the Son of God to earth.

When the first man and woman were made by God and placed on this earth, God wanted the joy of loving them and of having them love and obey Him. While that is the way it was in the beginning, it was not like that for long. Shortly the man and woman determined to have their own way. They refused to obey God. Wanting one's own way instead of God's way is sin. And, like the first man and woman, every person who has ever lived has chosen to have his/her own way. That sin separates us from God. Because of our sin, we are afraid of God.

But the Holy One loves us. Even though He hates our sin (see Proverbs 6:16-19), He loves us. So He planned a way for man to have his sin forgiven. He sent His perfect, only Son, the Lord Jesus Christ, to earth to show us what God is like. The Son of God showed us how we should live.

Show Illustration #6

And then the Lord Jesus died. His death was different, however. You remember that before this time, God had required that an animal should suffer the punishment for man's sin. The punishment for sin is death. God had allowed the animal to be the substitute for the person who had sinned. Although God had accepted animal sacrifices for hundreds of years, those sacrifices never took away sin. For each time a person sinned, another animal had to be sacrificed.

When the Son of God died, He took upon Himself once and for all, all the sin of all the world. (See John 3:16; Hebrews 10:11, 12.) He was "The Lamb [sacrifice] of God." (See John 1:29, 36.) He took all of your sins upon Himself. (See 1 Peter 2:24.) He could do this because He is the Son of God. He had come to earth not only to show us what God is like but He had come also to die for you . . . for me . . . for every person who would ever live. He took the punishment that we deserve!

3. CHRIST PROVED HE IS THE SON OF GOD BY RISING FROM THE DEAD
1 Corinthians 15:3-4

Show Illustration #7

How do we know that He is the Son of God? Because He did not stay dead. He rose again! (See 1 Corinthians 15:3, 4.) He commanded that those who know Him should tell others about Him. (See Matthew 28:18-20.) And that is the reason we are having this lesson. I want you to know that the Lord Jesus Christ is the Son of God. He loves you–loves you so much that He left God the Father and the beauties of Heaven to come and live here on earth. Then He died–died for *you*. Because He is the Son of God, He did not stay dead. He arose.

4. CHRIST WENT UP IN THE CLOUDS TO BE WITH GOD THE FATHER
Acts 1:9-11

Show Illustration #8

After His resurrection, the Lord Jesus went up in the clouds to Heaven. There He is with God the Father. At this very moment, He is waiting for you to believe Him.

What is it that you must believe? Believe that the Lord Jesus is the Son of God. Believe that when He died, He took the punishment for your sin. "He that believeth on the Son hath everlasting life: and he that believeth not the Son shall not see life; but the wrath of God abideth on him" (John 3:36).

Do you believe that the Lord Jesus is the Son of God? Do you believe that He loves you? He proved it by dying for you. He doesn't ask you to *understand* all of this. He says you must *believe* it. He wants you to turn to the living and true God from idols.

How can you know that all of this is true? Because the eternal God caused a Book to be written. That Book (the Bible) explains what God is like. It tells about His Son who came from God. It tells us this and much, much more. In our next lesson we are going to learn about that Book. Until then, repeat to yourself this wonderful truth: "The Lord Jesus, the Son of God, loves me. He died for me. He wants me to believe Him."

NOTE TO THE TEACHER
The Bible scroll shown on the front cover of this volume contains Isaiah 53:6 in Hebrew.

Lesson 3
THE BOOK OF GOD

NOTE TO THE TEACHER

If at all possible, your students should make notebooks. These may be very simple. The main points of each lesson should be written down. The students--either in class or at home--could be encouraged to make simple drawings that will help them to remember the lesson. They will be able to use their notebooks to tell the lesson to someone else.

We are told that we remember five times more of what we *hear* and *see* than of what we *hear* only. And we remember nine times more of what we *do*, hear and see! So the doing (making of notebooks and telling the lesson to others) is important.

Before teaching this lesson, you should fully explain the memory verse: *"Ye turned to God from idols to serve the living and true God."* (1 Thessalonians 1:9b)

Many, many people since time began have worshiped idols–gods made by their own hands. This was true in Thessalonica. However, when the people in that city heard of the true God of Heaven and of His Son, the Lord Jesus Christ, they destroyed their idols. And it could be said to them: "Ye [you] turned to God from idols to serve the living and true God."

Could it be said that *you* have turned to God from idols? Have you begun to serve the living and true God? The purpose of these lessons is to help you to do that. The true and living God of Heaven wants you to know Him. You must believe that the Lord Jesus Christ is His Son. Only if you believe that He died, taking the punishment for your sin, can you have forgiveness of sin. What is the final result of the forgiveness of sin? When life is over the forgiven sinner will live forever with God and His Son in His home, Heaven. In our next lesson we'll learn about the home of God.

Scripture to be studied: All verses mentioned in the text.

The *aim* of the lesson: To introduce the Bible as the true and living Word of God.

What your students should *know*: The Bible was written that we might believe that Jesus is the Christ, the Son of God, and that believing we might have life through His name. (See John 20:31.)

What your students should *feel*: An eagerness to learn what the Bible says to us.

What your students should *do*: Study Genesis 1:1; 1 Peter 1:16; 1 John 4:8; John 3:16. (If they do not have Bibles, please provide the verses for them.)

Lesson outline (for the teacher's and students' notebooks):

1. How we got our Bible, the Book of God (2 Peter 1:21).
2. The Book of God forgotten (2 Chronicles 34:1-7).
3. The Book of God found (2 Chronicles 34:8-15).
4. The Book of God obeyed (2 Chronicles 34:16-32).

THE LESSON

Have you been thinking of the other two lessons that we have had? I trust you have. Maybe you have been saying to yourself day after day:

(1) God is the Creator of all things . . . The Son of God is the Creator of all things.

(2) God is eternal. He always was. He always will be . . . The Son of God is eternal.

(3) God is holy–He has no sin . . . The Son of God is holy. He hates sin.

(4) God is love. He loves me . . . The Son of God loves me. He proved it by dying for my sin.

Having said those things, you may have wondered, *Are there two Gods–God the Father and God the Son?*

No! For in a most wonderful way (that God alone could think of or understand), God the Father and the Son are one God. This is difficult for us to understand. But we do not have to *understand* it. God wants us to *believe* it.

1. HOW WE GOT OUR BIBLE, THE BOOK OF GOD
2 Peter 1:21

Maybe you are thinking, *But how do we know these things to be true?*

Here is the answer to that: God has told us about them in His Book. And we are going to learn about that Book right now.

I have in my hand the Book of God. It is called *The Bible*. It is often called *The Word of God*. It is possible for us to hear words that are spoken and then to forget them. So, if God had spoken only, His words might have been forgotten. But the words of God are so important, and He has so much that He wants us to know, that He caused His words to be written down.

Show Illustration #9

Since God had the power to make the sun and trees and animals and people, He could have made a Book. But he did not choose to do that. Instead, He spoke to certain men who believed in Him, telling them to write down what He told them. At one time part of the Word of God was carved on tables of stone. (Show top drawing.) (See Exodus 24:12-18; 31:18; 34:1, 27-29; Deuteronomy 10:1-4.)

Later, the Word of God was written on scrolls. (Show center drawing.)

Today those words have been put into books like the one I hold. (See bottom drawing.)

In this one Book there are 66 books. Each has a different name. These 66 books were written by 40 different men. And it took them more than 1,500 years to write it all. Some of the men never knew each other. The men wrote in three different languages. Yet the writings gave the message of God to all people of all time. The first 39 books were written before the Lord Jesus came to earth. Those books are known as the *Old Testament*. The 27 books which follow were written after the Lord Jesus was born. They are called the *New Testament*.

While some of the men who wrote were kings, others were very simple people. Some were fishermen. Another made tents. But God did not let one of these 40 writers make a mistake. God breathed His thoughts into each man. He gave them a special power by which they wrote exactly what God wanted them to write. He caused them to write all that He wanted us to know. There is no other book in all the world which has been formed in such a way. The Book of God is the one and only perfect Book.

2. THE BOOK OF GOD FORGOTTEN
2 Chronicles 34:1-7

Today it is possible for almost every person to have his/her own copy of the Word of God. In the beginning that was not so. Only one copy was carved on stone or written in a scroll. And that copy was kept in a safe place (the house of God). Once, when there may have been only five books written (the five books of Moses), the people had forgotten the Book of God.

It happened this way: Men and women who had worshiped the living and true God had turned from Him to idols. They had made idols of wood and stone and gold and silver, bowed down to them and prayed to them. Could those gods see the people or hear them as they prayed? No, they could not! And, because the people had turned to idols, they did not go to the house of God to worship Him. Therefore the building (the temple) began to fall down–the very temple made for the worship of the living and true God.

A young man who had become king of the land knew that it was wrong to worship idols. His father had done that. His grandfather had done that. But he (Josiah) determined to destroy the idols as soon as he could. He wanted his people to turn from idols to serve the living and true God.

Show Illustration #10

So the first thing that Josiah did was to order his servants to destroy all the idols and tear down the places where people had worshiped those idols. Not one was to be left!

3. THE BOOK OF GOD FOUND
2 Chronicles 34:8-15

Later, King Josiah commanded that the building where the living and true God had been worshiped was to be repaired. The men worked faithfully, hammering, cleaning, fixing.

Show Illustration #11

Suddenly one of them found something that had been lost for such a long time that the people had forgotten all about it. It was the one copy of the Word of God (the Books of the Law)!

4. THE BOOK OF GOD OBEYED
2 Chronicles 34:16-32

Show Illustration #12

They rushed the Word of God to the king. He listened carefully as it was read to him. He heard what you now know: that God is the Creator of everything. He learned that the eternal God is holy and hates sin. He saw with his own eyes what he had known in his heart: that it was sin to make idols and to pray to them instead of believing in the living and true God and praying to Him. He learned, too, that God is a God of love.

The king called his people together, young and old. He read to them the Word of God. Before them all he promised to serve the living and true God and to obey the words of the Book of God. And all of the people made the same promise that day. So, because the people turned to the living and true God from idols, the holy, loving God forgave them. (*Teacher:* Read all about this in 2 Kings 22 and 23:1-3 and in 2 Chronicles 34.) If you, like that young king, will learn to love and obey the Word of God, many others will follow your example.

Why do I believe that this Book of God is truly the Word of God? Let me tell you:

(1) MY EYES TELL ME. I open to the very first sentence and read, "In the beginning God created the heaven and the earth" (Genesis 1:1). I look around and see the sun and trees and people. I know they could not simply have happened. They had to be created by One who has all power.

(2) MY MIND TELLS ME. I turn to the middle of the Word of God and read, "Before the mountains were brought forth, or ever Thou hadst formed the earth and the world, even from everlasting to everlasting, Thou art God" (Psalm 90:2). My mind makes me realize that the One who made this wonderful world had to be eternal (everlasting). He had to be before the world He made.

(3) MY HEART TELLS ME. Near the end of the Book I read that God says, "Be ye holy; for I am holy" (1 Peter 1:16). And, knowing myself, I know that I am not without sin. The God who made me is without sin. I know I have done wrong things. God hates my sin. My heart tells me this.

(4) MY LIFE TELLS ME. Again I read in His Book, "God is love" (1 John 4:8). And " . . . . God so loved the world, that He gave His only begotten Son, that whosoever believeth in Him should not perish, but have everlasting life" (John 3:16). One day, even though I did not understand it, I believed that God loved me. I believed that the Lord Jesus Christ is the Son of God, and that He died, taking the punishment for my sin. I asked Him to forgive my sin. I received Him as my Saviour. And my life was changed. I am so sure that this Book is the Word of God, that I want you to know the Book and the living and true God of the Book.

Why was the Word of God written? It tells us " . . . That ye might believe that Jesus is the Christ, the Son of God; and that believing ye might have life through His name" (John 20:31).

What kind of "life" do we receive when we believe in the Lord Jesus? The same kind of life that He has–eternal life! That means we will live forever and forever with Him in His wonderful home, Heaven. You will want to learn about that home in our next lesson.

NOTE TO THE TEACHER

If your students can read (and if you have a copy of the Bible in their language), let them read for themselves the verses in the last section. Or if there are more than can read from *your* Bible, print the verses on paper, on a board, or if necessary, on the ground. Let the living Book speak for itself!

Lesson 4
THE HOME OF GOD

Scripture to be studied: Revelation 1:9-18; 4:1-6; 5:11-13; 21:1-4, 25

The *aim* of the lesson: To explain how to get to Heaven.

What your students should *know*: Jesus Christ has made it possible for them to get to Heaven by believing in Him.

What your students should *feel*: A desire to receive Jesus as Saviour.

What your students should *do*: Believe in Jesus as the Son of God and receive Him as Saviour.

Lesson outline (for the teacher's and students' notebooks):
1. Jesus returns to God in Heaven (Acts 1:9).
2. Heaven is a beautiful place (Revelation 4:1-6; 5:11-13).
3. People from every nation will be in Heaven (Revelation 7:9-12).
4. Everything is perfect in Heaven (Revelation 21:1-4, 25).

NOTE TO THE TEACHER

How beautiful Heaven must be! Imagine living there forever and forever and forever! This is the blessing of those who have believed in the Lord Jesus Christ as the Son of God, and trusted Him as sin-bearer.

In reviewing the memory verse, ask questions to see if they really understand what it means when it is said of some,

Ye have turned to God from idols to serve the living and true God. (1 Thessalonians 1:9b)

Ask your students if they have "turned to God." Make certain they understand that the only way to turn to Him is by believing that the Lord Jesus is the Son of God and that He died, taking the punishment for their sin. If they believe this, if they ask for forgiveness of sin, they can have the assurance of life everlasting.

REVIEW

The living God has given us His Word, the Bible. No other Book is as wonderful as the Word of God.

Let us see how much we remember of our last lesson.

1. How many men did God choose to write His Word? *(40)*
2. How did the men know what to write? *(God breathed His thoughts into them.)*
3. Did the men make any mistakes as they wrote? *(No!)*
4. Why was the Word of God written? *(. . .That ye might believe that Jesus is the Christ, the Son of God; and that believing ye might have life through His name. John 20:31)*

THE LESSON
1. JESUS RETURNS TO GOD IN HEAVEN
Acts 1:9

The Bible tells us about God, about His Son, and about Heaven, the home of God. Heaven is a beautiful, wonderful place–more wonderful than we can imagine. But because God wants us to live in His home with Him, we want to know as much about it as we can. That is why we are having this lesson.

When the Lord Jesus lived here on earth, He had 12 disciples (followers) who worked with Him. They had seen Him heal the blind, make sick people well, and even bring dead people back to life!

They had seen the Lord Jesus die on a cross. While they did not understand it at first, they later realized that He was the Lamb of God, taking upon Himself the death punishment for all people who had ever lived or ever would live. Because He is the Son of God, He did not stay dead. He rose again. And His disciples saw Him with their own eyes. They knew Him then as their Lord and their God. (See John 20:28.)

After the Lord Jesus had risen from the dead, He explained that the Word of God, even that which was written hundreds of years before He lived, told about Him. (Read Luke 24:27, 44, 45.) "Yes," He said, "it was written long ago that I must suffer and die and rise again from the dead on the third day. This is the message that should be taken to all nations: *'There is forgiveness of sins for all who turn to Me.'*" (See Luke 24:46-48.)

Show Illustration #13

Forty days after He had risen from the dead, as the Lord Jesus was talking with His disciples, He suddenly began to rise into the air. Higher and higher He went until a cloud covered Him and the disciples couldn't see Him. The Lord Jesus had left this world and returned to His Father and His glorious home in Heaven!

2. HEAVEN IS A BEAUTIFUL PLACE
Revelation 4:1-6; 5:11-13

Show Illustration #14

As the disciples stared into the sky, two men dressed in white stood by them. They asked the disciples, "Why do you stand there looking up at the sky? This same Jesus, which is taken up from you into Heaven, will come back in the same way as you saw Him go into Heaven." Imagine that! They must have remembered then the promise that He had made: "I go to prepare a place for you . . . I will come again and receive you unto Myself that where I am, there ye may be also" (John 14:2, 3).

He, the sinless Son of God, had died for the sin of the world. He had proved He was the Son of God by rising from the dead. Now He had gone back to His Father God in His beautiful home, Heaven. He would someday return to take all of His own to be with Him in Heaven.

Heaven . . . what is it like? Those disciples wondered about that. Have you wondered about it? The Book of God tells us about the home of God. One of the disciples of the Lord Jesus (John), was punished for telling people about the Son of God. The people who punished him sent him to a lonely island called Patmos. Though he was alone on Patmos Island, God was with him. (See Revelation 1:9, 10.)

God did a very special thing for John while he was on Patmos. He let him see what Heaven was like. Because God breathed upon John, John wrote down what he saw. And that is part of the Word of God–the last book of the Bible (Revelation).

John saw the Lord Jesus in Heaven. He looked more glorious than He had ever looked on earth. "I am the living One," Jesus said. "I was dead, but now I am alive for ever and ever" (Revelation 1:18).

John also saw the throne of God. Around the throne was a beautiful rainbow and thousands of angels. The angels cried out: "The Lamb [they knew the Lord Jesus Christ as the Lamb of God] who was killed is worthy to receive power, and riches, and wisdom, and strength, and honor, and glory, and blessing!" (Revelation 4:5-6; 5:11-13)

3. PEOPLE FROM EVERY NATION WILL BE IN HEAVEN
Revelation 7:9-12

Show Illustration #15

Then John saw a great crowd of people–so great that they could not be counted. They had come from every nation, every tribe, and every language on earth, and stood before the throne and before the Lamb. The people were dressed in white robes. They held palm branches in their hands and called out together: "Our salvation comes from God who sits on the throne, and from the Lamb." Then the angels and people together praised God the Father and Jesus Christ, His Son. All remembered that the Son of God is the Lamb of God, the One who died for the sin of the world.

4. EVERYTHING IS PERFECT IN HEAVEN
Revelation 21:1-4, 25

John heard a shout from the throne: "Look! The home of God . . . God will wipe away all tears from their eyes. There will be no more death, no more sorrow, no more crying or pain or sickness. And there shall be no more night" (Revelation 21:1-4, 25).

Show Illustration #16a

Imagine that! There will never be a toothache in Heaven. There will not be any ache of any kind!

Show Illustration #16b

There will never be any famine in Heaven.

Show Illustration #16c

There will never be any accidents, any cuts or bruises in the home of God. No one will ever hurt him or herself in any way.

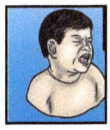

Show Illustration #16d

There will never be any crying in Heaven.

Show Illustration #16e

Do you see the sore on the foot? There will not be anything like that in God's home. There is no sickness there, no pain. These are the promises of God which John wrote down in the Book of God.

Best of all, there will never be any sin in the home of God. There will be no lying, no stealing, no anger or any such thing. In His home will be all of those whose names are written in the Lamb's Book of Life. (That is a special book in Heaven in which are written the names of all those who receive the Lord Jesus Christ as Saviour.)

Heaven is the home of God. He, the Creator, made it. (See Psalm 96:5.) His Son is there now preparing places for those who believe in Him. (See John 14:1-3.)

Heaven will be forever and forever and forever. Those who have the eternal life of God (received by believing in the Son of God) will live in Heaven forever.

Heaven is a holy place. There is no sin there. No suffering, no tears are there.

Heaven is a place of love, for it is the home of the God of love. The Lord Jesus, who proved His love for you by taking the punishment of death which you deserve, is there in Heaven.

God the Father and God the Son want you to be in Heaven with them. If you have believed that the Lord Jesus is the Son of God, if you have believed that He died for your sin, and if you have received the Lord Jesus Christ, then your name is written in the Lamb's Book of Life. That means that Heaven is your future home.

If you have not received the Lord Jesus as your Saviour, you may do so right now. Then you will be among those who have "turned to God from idols to serve the living and true God."

NOTE TO THE TEACHER

By now your students should have a number of things written (or pictured) in their notebooks. They should refer to them often so that the truths will be in their hearts permanently

As you continue using these volumes, you may want to refer to these first lessons again and again.

www.ingramcontent.com/pod-product-compliance
Lightning Source LLC
Chambersburg PA
CBHW060807090426
42736CB00002B/186